POWER OF MONEY

A Beginner's Guide to Financial Planning

MUGUGU BEAUDUIN

The Power of Money.

A beginner's guide to Financial Planning.

Copyright © 2023 by The Mugugu Company Inc.

All rights reserved. Except for use in a review, the reproduction or utilization of this work in any form by any electronic, mechanical, or other means, now known or hereafter invented, including xerography, photocopying, and recording, and in any information storage and retrieval system, is forbidden without the written permission of the publisher.

Table of Contents

DISCLAIMER 4

INTRODUCTION 6

CHAPTER 1 7
   Understanding Financial Planning 8

CHAPTER 2 12
   Setting Personal and Financial Goals 13

CHAPTER 3 16
Creating a Financial Plan 17

CHAPTER 4 19
   Managing Debt 20

CHAPTER 5 22
   Investing Wisely 23

CHAPTER 6 26
   Build Wealth Over Time 27

CHAPTER 7 31
   Tax Planning 32
   Different income, different taxes 35

CHAPTER 8 40

- Retirement Planning 42
- Do your own research 42
- Spend less, make more 43

CHAPTER 9 52
- Insurance Planning 53

CHAPTER 10 57
- Estate Planning 58

CHAPTER 11 62
- Avoiding Common Financial Mistakes 63

CHAPTER 12 65
- Putting It All Together 66

DISCLAIMER

This book was written mostly for Canadians although similar knowledge can also be applied to the U.S. The purpose of this book is to provide a general understanding of how money works in Canada, the financial concepts to know for investing, and information about those financial concepts. This book is not intended to give financial advice on investments, financial services nor taxes. Neither the author nor any other persons associated with this book may be held liable for any damages that may occur from the contents of this book. This book is not a substitute for professional advice. Readers are encouraged to seek financial advice from qualified professionals. All examples are hypothetical and are for illustration purposes only.

INTRODUCTION

In Canada, most people face a variety of financial challenges. According to several popular news sources in Ontario, it's estimated that 47% of the country lives paycheque to paycheque. That's more than 17 million people. Many are burdened by student loans, struggle to find affordable housing, and face an uncertain job market. However, with proper financial planning, Canadians can still achieve their financial goals. This book will provide a roadmap for people to reach their financial goals in the Canadian economy, with the help of financial planning. We will cover the basics of financial planning, such as setting financial goals, creating a budget, managing debt, and investing wisely.

CHAPTER

1

"Know your worth without the value of money"

Magaga Beaudain

Understanding Financial Planning

Financial planning is essential for everyone, especially young people who are starting their careers and building their lives. In the Canadian economy, most people have a range of financial goals that they need to achieve to secure their future but don't know how to go about it. This book is designed to help people reach their financial goals through financial planning.

Financial planning is the process of creating a roadmap for your financial future. It involves setting financial goals and creating a plan to achieve those goals. Financial planning can help you make informed decisions about your money, and it can help you build wealth over time.

To begin your financial planning journey, you must first assess your current financial situation. This involves understanding your income, expenses, assets, and debts. By having a clear picture of your finances, you can determine how much you can save and invest towards your financial goals.

I'm going to ask you some questions and would like you to ask yourself these questions too.

1. How much do I value my self worth?
2. Do I believe in myself?
3. How can I surround myself with people who encourage me?

4. What positive habits can I develop to improve my self worth?
5. What work am I putting in to achieve my personal and financial goals?
6. Are my spending habits depleting my financial health?

Don't be afraid to spend time with yourself. Ask yourself hard questions and be honest. Discovering yourself is part of the financial planning journey. During self-discovery, you'll find out what you're comfortable with and what you're not comfortable with. Believe in yourself. You have your own best interest so don't be afraid to exercise different ways to learn and to boost your confidence so that you can become better at planning for the future ahead of you.

CHAPTER

2

"Don't count the days, make the days count."

— Muhammad Ali

Setting Personal and Financial Goals

The first step to reaching your personal goals and financial goals is to set them. You should have both short-term and long-term goals. Short-term goals are those that can be achieved within a year or less and long-term goals are those that take several years or more to achieve.

An example of a short term financial goal would be paying off a credit card or saving for a trip. An example of a long term financial goal would be buying a house or saving for retirement.

An example of a personal short-term goal is to start exercising regularly, at least three times a week, for 30 minutes each session. An example of a long-term goal is to achieve career advancement. This might include getting a promotion to a higher position, completing additional education or training to advance in your field, or even starting your own business.

The next step is writing down your financial goals on a piece of paper. These goals should be specific, measurable, achievable, relevant, and time-bound. An example of a specific, measurable, achievable, relevant, and time-bound goal would be "By working 40 hours a week from January to December, after all expenses, I'll have an emergency fund of $5000." Always carry the paper with you to remind you of your goal and to invite that energy into your space.

When setting your goals, it is important to consider your personal values and priorities. Your goals should align with what you want to achieve in life, and they should be meaningful to you.

After you've set financial goals, create a plan to achieve those goals, and regularly review and monitor your performance.

CHAPTER 3

"Don't be the individual they want you to be. Be the individual they'd never thought you'd become."

Mugugu Beaudoin

Creating a Financial Plan

Once you have established your goals, the next step is creating a financial plan. A financial plan outlines the steps you need to take to achieve your goals. It should include a budget, an investment plan, and a debt repayment plan.

Budgeting is an essential part of planning. It involves tracking your income and expenses and allocating your money towards your financial goals. A budget can help you stay on track and avoid overspending.

Create a budget and stick to it. By creating a budget, you can see where your money is going and not going. It will help you identify areas where you can save money and areas that will allow you to spend a bit more. You can use a variety of tools, such as spreadsheets on Microsoft Excel or budgeting apps. Make sure to create a budget that works for you.

CHAPTER

4

"Positive thinking manifests positive actions."

— Magagu Beaudain

Managing Debt

Debt can be a significant obstacle to reaching your financial goals. It's important to manage your debt wisely, so you don't end up paying more than you need to in interest charges. There are several strategies for managing debt, including consolidating debt, paying off high-interest debt first, and negotiating with creditors.

Debt repayment is also a critical part of planning. High levels of debt can prevent you from achieving your financial goals, so it is important to create a plan to pay off your debts as quickly as possible.

Managing debt takes time and effort, but with a little discipline and a solid plan, you can get back on track and become debt-free.

Prioritize your debts: my suggestion is to make a list of all your debts and prioritize them by amounts owed. Focus on paying off the debts with the lowest balance first. That way once it's paid off, you'll feel a sense of accomplishment.

Seek professional help: If you're struggling to manage your debt, consider seeking help from a credit counseling service or a financial advisor.

CHAPTER

5

"It may cost you to invest in yourself but nothing is more expensive than a missed opportunity"

Mugugu Beaudwin

Investing Wisely

Investing is another important component of financial planning. Investing can help you grow your wealth over time, but it also involves risks. It is important to understand the risks and rewards of different investment options before investing your money.

It's essential to invest wisely to ensure that your money is working for you. There are many different types of investments, including stocks, bonds, mutual funds, real estate, etc. It's important to research your investment options and consult with a financial advisor before making any investment decisions.

Investing is an important way to build wealth over the long term. A great resource for learning about investments would be '*The Power of Money, Beginners Guide to Investing'*. It will provide you with the basics of what you need to know before you decide to invest.

<u>Building Good Financial Habits</u>

Think of your financial habits like a diet, if you eat nothing but fast food, fried foods, candy, and desserts, you won't be very healthy and are likely to develop health issues. On the other hand, if you eat a lot of fruits, vegetables and have a balanced diet, you are less likely to have health issues. Reaching your financial goals requires discipline and good financial habits. You should strive to save money, avoid unnecessary debt, and invest wisely. By building good financial habits, you can achieve your financial goals in the time span you set out for yourself. You'll ensure your financial future and the future of your family.

CHAPTER

6

"Is your money working for you or are you working for your money?"

Mugugu Beaudain

Build Wealth Over Time

Building wealth is a long-term process that requires discipline and patience. One of the best ways to build wealth is to diversify your portfolio with multiple assets such as stocks, real estate, certain watches, etc. This can help you earn returns that exceed inflation over the long term.

Another way to build wealth is to take advantage of tax-sheltered accounts, such as Registered Retirement Savings Plans (RRSPs) and Tax-Free Savings Accounts (TFSAs). These accounts allow you to save and invest your money while deferring taxes.

Saving

In order to build wealth, you're going to need to save. Saving is an essential part of financial planning. Saving money is important for building financial stability, achieving future goals, preparing for retirement, and reducing financial stress. It's a critical component of a healthy financial plan and can help you achieve greater financial freedom and peace of mind.

Saving money is also important for several reasons:

Emergency Fund: Unexpected events, such as a job loss, medical emergency, or home repair, can arise at any time. Having savings set aside for such emergencies can provide you with a financial safety net and help you avoid going into debt.

Future Expenses: You may have future expenses that you need to save for, such as a down payment on a house, your child's college education, or a dream vacation. Saving money regularly can help you achieve these goals without resorting to loans or credit.

Retirement: Saving for retirement is crucial to ensure that you can maintain your standard of living and cover your expenses when you're no longer working. The earlier you start saving, the more time your money has to grow, and the less you'll need to save each year to reach your retirement goals.

Peace of Mind: Having money set aside can give you peace of mind and reduce stress about your finances. It can provide a sense of security, knowing that you have a cushion to fall back on in case of unexpected expenses or financial setbacks.

CHAPTER

7

"Know the difference between enjoying your youth and destroying your future."

Unknown

Tax Planning

Taxes are a fact of life, but with proper planning, Canadians can minimize their tax liability.

Here are a few tips:

Maximize your RRSP contributions: Registered Retirement Savings Plan (RRSP) contributions are tax-deductible, which means that the money you contribute to your RRSP can be subtracted from your taxable income, reducing your tax bill. Consider contributing the maximum amount each year to your RRSP to take advantage of this tax benefit.

Consider a TFSA: A Tax-Free Savings Account (TFSA) allows you to save money tax-free, meaning that any investment gains and withdrawals are not taxed. This can be a great way to reduce your tax bill over the long term, especially if you expect to be in a higher tax bracket in the future.

Take advantage of tax credits: There are many tax credits available in Canada that can help reduce your tax bill, such as the child care expense deduction, the disability tax credit, and much more. Make sure you are aware of all the tax credits you may be eligible for and take advantage of them when filing your taxes.

Consider incorporating your business: If you are self-employed or run a small business, incorporating your business can provide you with significant tax benefits. This is because incorporated businesses are taxed at a lower rate than individuals.

Work with a tax professional: Tax planning can be complex, especially as you accumulate wealth and your tax situation becomes more complicated. Consider working with a tax professional who can help you develop a personalized tax plan that takes into account your unique financial situation and goals.

Different income, different taxes

In Canada, income from your investment accounts can come in different forms. The most common include interest, dividends, and capital gains. Dividends paid on shares of stock issued by Canadian corporations receive more favourable tax treatment since this income benefits from the federal dividend tax credit. Investments like GIC's or savings deposit accounts are taxed at the highest marginal tax rate. Below I've listed accounts that taxed immediately, tax deferred, and have a tax advantage:

Taxed Immediately	Taxed Deferred	Tax-Free

Chequings	Registered retirement income funds (RRIFs)	Tax-Free Savings Account (TFSA)
Savings	registered retirement savings plan (RRSP)	
Bonds	registered education savings plan (RESP)	
GIC	Registered Disability Savings Plan (RDSP)	
Mutual Funds		
Stocks		
Non registered accounts		

Registered Retirement Income Funds (RRIF)

A Registered Retirement Income Fund is an account that gives you a steady income during retirement. Once you've reached the age of 71, you have to take out your RRSP money either in cash or transfer it to a RRIF.

Registered Education Savings Plan (RESP)

A Registered Education Savings Plan encourages investing in a child's future post-secondary education. Money put into a RESP is tax-sheltered until withdrawal. Government offers grant and bonds for RESP called the CESG (Canada Education Savings Grant). The government will match 20% on the first $2500 contributed annually.

Registered Disability Savings Plan (RDSP)

A Registered Disability Savings Plan is intended to help parents, people with disabilities, and people receiving assistance from family to save for their future financial security. Beneficiaries who are eligible for the DTC (Disability Tax Credit) are allowed to apply for grant or bond by December 31st of the year the beneficiary turns age 49.

Non-Registered Account

With a Non-Registered Account, investment income is taxed but withdrawals are not and have no contribution limits.

As per the Canadian Revenue Agency, these are the Federal tax brackets for individuals:

Annual Income (2023)	Tax Rates
0 to $53,359	15%
Over $53,359 to $107,717	20.5%
$107,717 to $165,430	26%
$165,430 to $235,675	29%
Over $235,675	33%

CHAPTER

8

"The time is always right to do what's right."

Martin Luther King Jr.

Retirement Planning

The higher the risk, the greater the potential reward. The lower the risk, the lower the potential reward. The way to hedge your funds is to learn as much as you can in order to diversify your portfolio of investments.

Do your own research

When investing, keep in mind that the statistics, share prices, dividend yields, rate of returns, and prime rates are all past information. Use it to your advantage and let it factor into your future decision-making.

Spend less, make more

Rome wasn't built overnight, neither is building a solid financial foundation. That's why taking the time to pay attention to your spending habits is super important. The less you spend, the more you can pay yourself. I've taken the time to list suggestions to help you attain the financial freedom you desire.

1. **Increase your streams of income.** Most people work a full-time job and find it difficult to keep up with the demand because they're trading their time for money. Find ways to multiply your time by making passive income. There are many ways to earn passive income, whether it's investing in dividend

stocks, making music, making YouTube videos, or setting up affiliate marketing links, find what works for you and focus on those skills. Don't limit yourself, the more streams of income you have, the more you'll multiply your time.

2. **Spend less.** Cut down on any unnecessary expenses. Go through your bank statement and see which purchases you can make less of in the future. Cut down on TV, screen time (hours spent looking at your phone), and other activities that might not be beneficial.

3. **Pay your debt.** If you have any loans, credit card debts, or even debts in collection, PAY THEM! By paying off your debt you will

increase your credit score, which will give you a better opportunity to obtain bigger loans in the future, like a mortgage.

4. **Have an end goal.** How much money is enough for you to retire? Have a specific goal in mind and work backward from that goal. With a lot of in-depth planning, risk-taking, hard work, and believing, it's possible to come to that evaluation in a much shorter time

5. **Make a Vision Board.** You have to be able to see and your future. Most people must see it to believe it. So, manifesting it into reality will make it more of a plan and not a dream.

6. **Work on your financial health.** Look into what you want to invest in. If you don't know where to start, try to find companies whose products you already own. Take Apple, for example, look up the company's news, what makes them so valuable, how long they've been in business, how well have they been performing over the years, etc. Keep in mind to put your money in an investment vehicle that is performing better than the current inflation rate. Don't be afraid to ask questions to make the best decisions possible. Make sure to invest your money long enough to let the compound interest build up your wealth. Finally, look for investments that have tax advantages.

Even though retirement may seem like a long way off, it's essential to start planning for it as early as possible. There are several retirement savings options in Canada:

Registered Retirement Savings Plan (RRSP)

This is the most common retirement account in Canada. A Registered Retirement Savings Plan is a type of savings account for retirement and an account to shelter your investments in. Money put into an RRSP is tax-sheltered until withdrawal. In addition, a contribution receipt will be given and can be used as an income tax deduction. An investor can contribute up to 18% of their previous years' income. Up to a maximum of $30 780 for the year 2023. RRSP contributions are subject to an annual contribution limit based on a percentage of your income, and there are penalties for over-contributing.

Tax-Free Savings Account (TFSA)

A Tax-Free Savings Account is a savings account that provides tax benefits for saving. Investment income, interest, dividends, and capital gains earned in a TFSA are tax-free. Fun fact, if you're over the age of majority and have never contributed to a TFSA, you can check the Canada Revenue Agency (CRA) website to check how much contribution room is available for you.

Registered Retirement Income Funds (RRIF)

A Registered Retirement Income Fund is an account that gives you a steady income during retirement. It is created by converting an RRSP or a locked-in retirement account (LIRA) into a RRIF. Withdrawals from a RRIF are taxed as income.

Locked-in Retirement Account (LIRA)

LIRA's are designed to hold pension funds transferred from a previous employer. The funds in a LIRA are locked-in, which means that they cannot be withdrawn until retirement age. Like RRSPs, investment earnings grow tax-free.

Registered Pension Plan (RPP)

This is a pension plan that is sponsored by an employer. Contributions to RPPs are tax-deductible, and investment earnings grow tax-free. The retirement income provided by an RPP is taxed as income.

Deferred Profit Sharing Plan (DPSP)

This is a retirement savings plan that is offered by some employers. Contributions to DPSPs are tax-deductible, and investment earnings grow tax-free. The retirement income provided by a DPSP is taxed as income.

Supplemental Retirement Savings Plan (SRSP)

This is a retirement savings plan that is offered by some employers. Contributions to SRSPs are not tax-deductible, but investment earnings grow tax-free. The retirement income provided by an SRSP is taxed as income.

It's important to start saving for retirement as early as possible to take advantage of the power of compound interest. Note that there may be limits and rules around each of these retirement accounts, and it's a good idea to consult with a financial advisor to determine which accounts are best suited to your financial situation and retirement goals.

CHAPTER 9

"Never be limited by other people's limited imaginations."

Dr. Mae Jemison

Insurance Planning

Insurance is another essential part of financial planning. This chapter will cover how to go about selecting the right insurance policies for your needs. It will also give tips on risk management that is associated with insurance planning.

Identify your insurance needs

The first step in insurance planning is to determine what types of insurance you need. Some common types of insurance in Canada include life insurance, disability insurance, health insurance, auto insurance, and home insurance. Assess your situation and determine which types of insurance are necessary for you and your family.

Research different insurance providers: Once you know what types of insurance you need, research different insurance providers in your town or province. Compare the coverage, premiums, and benefits offered by each provider to determine which one is best for you.

Choose the right coverage: It's important to choose the right coverage for your needs. For example, if you have dependents, you may want to consider purchasing life insurance with a higher coverage amount to ensure they are financially protected in the event of your death. If you own a home or a car, you may want to purchase insurance with comprehensive coverage to protect against damage and theft.

Set your budget: Insurance premiums can add up, so it's important to set a budget for your insurance coverage. Determine how much you can afford to pay each month for insurance and choose a policy that fits within your budget.

Review and update your policies regularly: Your insurance needs may change over time, so it's important to review and update your policies regularly. For example, if you have a child or purchase a new home, you may need to adjust your coverage accordingly.

Consider working with an insurance broker: If you are unsure about which insurance policies are right for you or if you want help navigating the insurance market, consider working with an insurance broker. Brokers can help you find the best policies for your needs and budget.

Stay informed: Stay up-to-date on changes in the insurance market and regulations. Keep an eye out for new policies or changes to existing policies that may benefit you. You can also consult with a financial advisor or insurance expert to stay informed about the latest developments in the industry.

CHAPTER

10

"Freeing yourself is one thing, acknowledging that freedom is another."

Magaga Beaudin

Estate Planning

Estate planning is often overlooked by young Canadians, but as scary as it may come across, it is an important part of financial planning. This chapter will cover the basics of estate planning and ensuring that your assets are distributed according to your wishes.

Determine your estate planning goals: The first step in estate planning is to determine your goals. This may include ensuring that your assets are distributed to your loved ones according to your wishes, minimizing estate taxes, or providing for the care of any dependents.

Make an inventory of your assets: Make a list of all your assets, including real estate, investments, bank accounts, retirement accounts, and personal property.

Choose your beneficiaries: Determine who you want to receive your assets when you pass away. This may include your spouse, children, other family members, or charitable organizations.

Choose an executor: Choose someone you trust to manage your estate when you pass away. This person will be responsible for paying off any debts, distributing assets to beneficiaries, and handling other estate-related tasks.

Write a will: A will is a legal document that outlines your wishes for the distribution of your assets after you pass away. It's important to work with a lawyer to ensure that your will is legally binding and meets all of the requirements of Canadian law. When writing your will, be sure to include your beneficiaries, executor, and any specific instructions for the distribution of your assets.

Consider other estate planning tools: In addition to a will, there are other estate planning tools that can help you achieve your goals. This may include setting up a trust to provide for the care of any dependents or to minimize estate taxes.

Review and update your plan regularly: It's important to review and update your estate plan regularly, especially if there are any major life changes, such as a marriage, divorce, birth of a child, or the acquisition of new assets. Be sure to update your will and other estate planning documents to reflect any changes in your wishes or circumstances.

Communicate your plan to your loved ones: It's important to communicate your estate plan to your loved ones so that they are aware of your wishes and can avoid any potential disputes or misunderstandings. Be sure to discuss your plan with your family members and other beneficiaries, and consider providing them with a copy of your will and other estate planning documents.

CHAPTER 11

"It isn't where you come from, it's where you're going that counts."

Ella Fitzgerald

Avoiding Common Financial Mistakes

There are several common financial mistakes that people should avoid. These include:

Overspending: Spending more money than you earn can lead to debt and financial stress.

Failing to save: Saving money is essential for achieving financial goals and building wealth.

Not investing: Investing can help you grow your wealth over time and beat inflation.

Ignoring debt: High levels of debt can prevent you from achieving your financial goals, so it is important to create a plan to pay off your debts as quickly as possible.

Failing to plan: Financial planning is essential for achieving your goals and building wealth.

CHAPTER 12

"Keep going. No matter what."

Reginald Lewis

Putting It All Together

In this final chapter, we will bring together all of the concepts covered in this book and provide a step-by-step guide to creating a comprehensive financial plan. We will also provide tips for staying on track and adjusting your plan as your financial situation changes.

Financial planning is essential for people who want to achieve their financial goals and build wealth over time. By assessing your current financial situation, setting financial goals, creating a financial plan, and avoiding common financial mistakes, you can take control of your financial future and achieve financial security. The key to success is discipline and patience. Stick to your plan and stay focused on your long-term goals, and you will be on the path to financial success.

Remember:

Set Personal and Financial Goals

Create a plan to reach those goals

Manage your debt

Invest wisely

Build your wealth over time

Plan for taxes

Plan for retirement

Plan for insurance

Prepare your estate documents

Avoid common financial mistakes

NOTES:

FIN

www.ingramcontent.com/pod-product-compliance
Lightning Source LLC
Chambersburg PA
CBHW070124230526
45472CB00004B/1405